D1408171

Jobs as GREEN BUILDERS and PLANNERS

ROSEN
PUBLISHING®
New York

Ann Byers

*To Cory, who builds beautiful houses for some people
and a wonderful home for my daughter and grandchildren*

Published in 2010 by The Rosen Publishing Group, Inc.
29 East 21st Street, New York, NY 10010

Library of Congress Cataloging-in-Publication Data

Byers, Ann.
Jobs as green builders and planners / Ann Byers. — 1st ed.
    p. cm. — (Green careers)
Includes bibliographical references and index.
ISBN 978-1-4358-3566-5 (library binding)
1. Environmental sciences — Vocational guidance — Juvenile literature.
2. Sustainable buildings — Juvenile literature. 3. Buildings —
Environmental aspects — Juvenile literature. I. Title.
GE60.B94 2010
690.023 — dc22

                                                                  2009015517

Manufactured in Malaysia
CPSIA Compliance Information: Batch #TW10YA: For Further Information contact Rosen Publishing, New York, New York at 1-800-237-9932

On the cover: Workers prepare native plantings for the 2.5-acre (10,117 square meter) green roof atop the California Academy of Sciences building in Golden Gate Park, San Francisco.

On the title page: Left: An architect drafts plans for a green building project, including the important landscaping elements that will maximize the complex's energy efficiency and eco-friendliness. Right: A building designer instructs the Bobcat operator on what needs to be done.

CONTENTS

Introduction

Imagine yourself as a guest at Gaia, a beautiful hotel in California's Napa Valley. From the moment you arrive, you can sense this hotel is different from most others. The seaside daisies and desert marigolds are beautiful, but something in the landscape is missing. Grass! There is no grass! Instead, the ground is covered with coyote brush and wild lilac—native vegetation that requires very little watering.

As you pull into the parking lot, notice the special vehicle stalls. Some have power outlets for electric cars, some are marked for hybrid vehicles, and others are reserved for carpooling vans. Something is different about

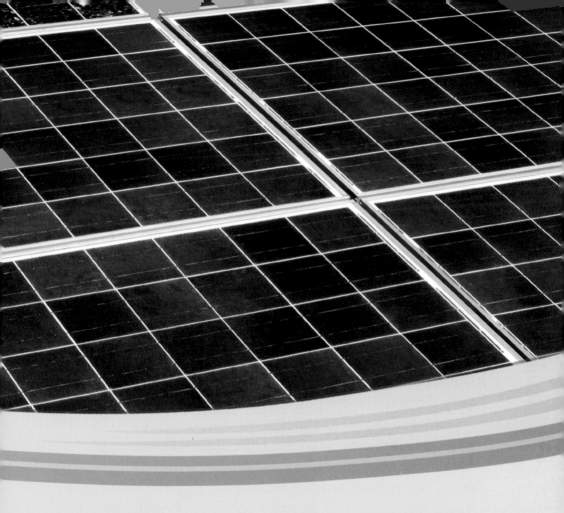

the sidewalks, too. Rather than the typical whitish-gray color of concrete, the cement has a slightly brown tinge.

Inside, you may be surprised at the unusual skylights in the lobby. They are solatubes, highly polished aluminum tubes that magnify and direct the sun's rays. The covers you see over them are diffusers, which are needed to soften the concentrated light.

As you stroll through the hallways and into the restrooms, take a good look at the floor. The tiles are not all the same size. You might notice colored flecks or crackly lines in some of them. That is because they are all made of recycled materials. Did you see the restroom brighten up as you entered? A motion sensor turns lights on when someone enters. In case you forget to turn the lights off when you leave, an occupancy sensor detects when the room is unoccupied and shuts off the unneeded lights. While you are in the restroom, take a look at the toilets. They let you choose between two different flushes, depending on whether you need a moderate amount of water or just a little. And the urinals are waterless.

If you are sensitive to odors, you will probably notice that typical scents are missing in this hotel. None of the types of paints, adhesives, sealants, and other materials that give recently constructed buildings their distinctively "new" smell are present in this hotel. Neither will you detect chemical cleaning agents. The air you are breathing is very clean. Even the furniture is free of harmful chemicals.

Are you ready to check out your guest room? You will see some features you don't find in most hotels. Motion sensors control the room's temperature. Everything in the room is made of natural materials: curtains, linens, even the furniture. And of course each room has its own recycling bin. In addition, all the paper products throughout the hotel are made of recycled materials.

The Gaia in Napa Valley is a green hotel—the first green hotel in the United States to receive a gold rating for its friendliness to the environment. Large displays and touch screens in the lobby show how much the hotel is saving in water and electricity. They also show how much of the heat-trapping greenhouse gas carbon dioxide (CO_2) is being emitted into the atmosphere. Building the hotel was a huge undertaking that took more than two years and many, many people. It took planners—architects who designed how the buildings would look and different kinds

The 113-room Gaia Napa Valley Hotel and Spa in American Canyon, California, is the first hotel in the United States to earn a gold rating for sustainable building. The name "Gaia" means "Mother Earth" in Greek.

of engineers who figured out how to make those designs work. It took builders—carpenters, tile workers, electricians, plumbers, and others—who turned the design into a physical reality. It took managers—a project manager who made sure all the elements and systems worked together well and a construction manager who supervised the builders. It took consultants—people who were experts in ecology, energy conservation, and waste management—to see that everything was as "green" as it could be. And it took beautifiers—landscapers, interior designers, and furniture makers—who, in a sense, "made the house a home."

Chapter One

What Makes a Building Green?

In the not too distant past, people built homes without much thought to the effect their building might have on the environment. If they needed wood, they cut down a tree. They didn't think about the next person who wanted to construct a home. After all, there were plenty more trees. But every year our planet has more people on it than the year before. And every year people need and

The University of Memphis built this TERRA house. "TERRA" stands for "technologically and environmentally responsive residential architecture." The house incorporates the LEED guidelines of the U.S. Green Building Council.

use more of the earth's resources. Builders have begun to consider doing their work in such a way as to save some of the earth's precious and dwindling resources for future generations.

Sustainable Building

Green construction is sustainable building. It is building in a way that sustains, or keeps, natural resources so they will be there for other people to use, both now and for generations to come. Sustainable building is called "green building" because it protects the natural environment and restores what it takes out of it. Green builders use terms such as "eco-efficient" and "eco-friendly." These terms indicate that they use the natural resources in the environment without creating a negative impact on the ecosystem.

What makes green building different from other types of construction is its emphasis on sustaining the environment. Green building sustains the environment—is eco-friendly—in two ways. First, it uses natural resources efficiently so they are not wasted. Second, it manages the resources in ways that result in little or no harm to the environment or to human health. Green buildings are different from traditional buildings in their materials, their production and management of energy, and their management of water.

Materials

All building materials start with natural resources. Wood comes from trees, adobe bricks and stucco are made from sand and other natural materials, and steel is made

9

from iron. Some resources are renewable. These are items that can be made again, or renewed. Trees, like all plants, can be replaced in the natural environment. Other resources, such as sand and iron, are nonrenewable; once they are used, they are gone forever. Using nonrenewable resources depletes rather than sustains the environment. Therefore, green building uses materials made from renewable resources whenever possible.

Resources are renewed at different rates. An oak tree takes 120 years to reach maturity, whereas bamboo takes only three to seven years. Green building uses building materials made from rapidly renewable resources—plants that can be renewed within only ten years.

One way to avoid depleting natural resources is to use materials that have already been made from those resources. Green builders sometimes install posts, doors, bricks, and other items salvaged or reused from other building projects. They also use recycled materials such as bottlestone, which is made of ground pieces of scrap glass.

The materials in a green building are not only natural or recycled; they also do not harm the environment or people. Many of the products used in ordinary construction contain volatile organic compounds (VOCs). These are chemicals that are emitted into the air as gaseous vapors. They are what you smell in paints, adhesives, sealants, and many cleaning products. They are even in carpets and furniture. VOCs are hazardous to animals and humans. They may cause minor eye, nose, or throat irritation. In severe cases, they can cause cancer and organ damage. Green builders choose materials that have few if any VOCs.

Workmen are removing wood from the side of this Kentucky barn. They work for a company that salvages wood, restores it, and makes it into hardwood flooring.

Green planners have to think about more than what the material is made of and what emissions it might produce. They also have to consider what it takes to get the material to the construction site. If a builder in Ohio buys flooring in California, quite a bit of diesel fuel is expended trucking the material to the construction site. And diesel fuel is a nonrenewable resource. Diesel fuel also emits harmful chemicals and gases into the atmosphere. The positives in using the flooring are outweighed by the negatives in transporting it. So green builders try to use materials that are produced within 500 miles (805 kilometers) of the construction site.

Energy

Every building requires energy in both its construction and its operation. Traditional builders use energy that is generated though the burning of fossil fuels: coal, oil, or natural gas. These are nonrenewable resources that were created centuries ago from decayed plant and animal life. Generating energy from fossil fuels not only uses up resources. Extracting them from the earth also tears up ecosystems and releases harmful gases and pollutants into the atmosphere.

Green builders produce and use electrical and thermal (heat) energy from renewable resources. These resources may be the sun's rays (solar power), wind (wind power), water (hydroelectricity), plants (biofuels), and heat found deep in the earth (geothermal heat). They use this renewable energy to heat, cool, and light buildings and to power equipment. Large green projects often produce more electrical power than they actually need. In these cases, they send the excess to the local power grid that serves the entire community.

In addition to producing energy on-site when possible, green builders must use energy efficiently, without wasting any. One way they do this is by designing buildings that need less energy for their systems and operations. For example, deciding which direction a building will face, where to install windows, and where to plant trees affects how much heating and lighting that building will require. A wide range of energy conservation features such as glazed windows, tankless water heaters, and occupancy sensors are also built into green buildings.

These pipes hold geothermal water—hot water that comes from far beneath the earth's surface. The water is being pumped to a power station, where its heat serves as the power source for generating electricity. After it is used, the water is returned to the earth.

Water

Energy conservation is important to our way of life, but water conservation is critical to our very survival. Water is a renewable resource, but at present, water is being used much more rapidly than it is being restored. In the United States, we use 3.7 billion gallons (14 trillion liters), more than we return to the environment every year (according to the *LEED-NC for New Construction Reference Guide*). Sustainable building finds ways to reduce the amount of water that is wasted.

One water resource that is often wasted is rainwater. Rainwater is not potable—it can not be used for drinking—but it can be used for flushing toilets and watering plants. Some green builders design systems that collect rainwater from roofs, store it in tanks, and use it for these purposes. Others let the rain fall onto "green roofs"—gardens planted on the tops of buildings. Green builders often install permeable pavement—sidewalks and driveways made of material or of a design that allows water to trickle into the ground beneath them. This keeps much of the rainwater in the ecosystem.

Quite a bit of water is used in showering, washing hands, and washing clothes. Wastewater from these activities is called gray water. It is not potable, but it can be treated and reused. Green builders design systems that filter gray water through sand, plants, or other natural processes. Buildings that have laundry facilities, such as hotels, may have systems that permit them to filter and reuse the water used in their washing machines.

One of the most obvious places to conserve water is in a project's landscaping. Green builders decorate grounds

At Chicago's Museum of Science and Natural History, a rain barrel collects water, which can then be used in the building's plumbing system or to irrigate plants, or it can be returned to the ground.

with plants that are native to the area, plants that can survive on whatever amounts of rainfall are common to the locale. They plan carefully, situating the buildings, trees, and other plants to provide the right amount of sun and shade for each type of plant they select. If the plants need watering, stored rainwater or gray water is recycled for irrigation.

Recycling

Green builders not only use recycled materials, they also recycle the waste their activities generate. Every construction site has leftover wood, concrete, wallboard, cardboard, and other materials. Almost every bit of it can be recycled. Extra boards, pipes, and light fixtures can be used by other contractors at other sites. Unused concrete and asphalt can be crushed and mixed with cement to create new concrete and paving materials. The mineral gypsum in scraps of drywall can be reclaimed and used in making new products. Wood waste can be combined with recycled plastic to form a composite lumber that is perfect for decks and fences.

Recycling building materials that would otherwise be discarded and wasted helps prevent the depletion of natural resources. It also keeps perfectly usable materials from being dumped into landfills, where they cause pollution and take hundreds or even thousands of years to decompose.

Measuring "Greenness"

As more and more people recognize the importance of protecting the natural environment, many are jumping

A Living Roof

The world's largest green roof sits atop the Ford Motor Company's River Rogue plant in Dearborn, Michigan. The truck manufacturing plant, rebuilt in 2003 with the help of Michigan State University, has 454,000 square feet (10.4 acres; 42,178 sq meters) of vegetation on its roof. Nine different varieties of sedum, a drought-resistant ground cover, hold the rain that falls on the roof, keeping storms from causing flooding. The plants absorb carbon dioxide, reducing greenhouse gases. The green roof provides insulation, lowering heating and cooling costs, and doubles the life of the roof. It is home to a variety of birds, including Canadian geese, mallard ducks, and killdeer.

on the "green" bandwagon. Companies are now making and advertising building products as eco-friendly. People are installing solar panels on their houses and adding low-flow showerheads. But how green do these additions make a building? How can you tell exactly how eco-friendly a product or a project is? The U.S. Green Building Council is a nonprofit group of representatives of more than 6,500 companies and organizations in the building industry. It established an objective rating system for measuring a building's "greenness." It is called Leadership in Energy and Environmental Design, or LEED.

The LEED rating system is the most widely used standard for determining how eco-friendly a construction project is. LEED has separate rating systems for different types of construction, such as new buildings, remodels, homes, and large developments. In general, the systems measure six elements of the design, building, and maintenance of construction projects. These are the six criteria by which a project will be rated for greenness:

Sustainable site: Where the project is located affects how well natural resources are protected.

Water efficiency: A green project must conserve water.

Energy and atmosphere: Green buildings must use less energy than others and use forms of energy that do not produce harmful emissions.

Materials and resources: What construction materials are made of, how they are processed, and how they get to the building site are all important considerations.

Indoor environmental quality: Indoor air is two to five times more polluted than outdoor air; green buildings have to improve indoor air quality.

Innovation in design: Green builders do not simply follow a set of rules. They are constantly looking for new and creative ways to be even greener.

The U.S. Green Building Council awards points in each of the six LEED categories. For example, in the rating system for new construction projects (as opposed to remodels or renovations), sixty-four core points are possible plus five extra credit points, for a total of sixty-nine points. The number of points awarded translates into a rating that indicates the level of greenness of the project:

26–32 points = Certified
33–38 points = Silver
39–51 points = Gold
52–69 points = Platinum

The green building industry is growing quickly. The number of new projects applying for LEED certification has grown more than 60 percent every year since 2006. According to the Georgia Municipal Association, the number grew by 80 percent in 2008. That means demand is rising for people who know how to plan and build green.

Chapter Two
Green Planners

In a truly green building, everything is related. A rainwater collection system on the outside may be needed to flush toilets inside, and a rooftop wind turbine may power lights in rooms beneath it. So all the people involved in the designing and building of the structure and its systems have to plan carefully and work together closely. Green buildings require entire teams of planners.

The typical process of planning a building or a complex of buildings begins something like this: An architect

This is an architect's design for an actual sustainable city being planned for construction near Seoul, Korea, called Gwanggyo. The hill-like buildings are designed to house seventy-seven thousand people as well as stores, offices, schools, and sports and entertainment centers.

produces an overall design, a master plan. Engineers figure out how to make the different parts of the plan work. Civil engineers decide how the building will be situated on the lot, where sidewalks and driveways will go, and how to control the flows of water and vehicular and foot traffic. Electrical engineers plan the wiring—where lights, major appliances, and outlets will be placed. Mechanical engineers design systems for heating, air-conditioning, and ventilation. Various architectural and engineering technicians pencil out the details so that the designers' visions can move from notes and drawings on paper to actual "brick-and-mortar" buildings.

The highest levels of planners—the architects and engineers—generally need to have college degrees as well as several years of experience. They also often have to be LEED accredited. That means they passed an exam demonstrating their knowledge of LEED standards. But many lower-level technician jobs are available to people who are just beginning to acquire skills in the building trades and industries.

Architects

Architects design buildings. They listen to what developers say they want, and they then produce detailed pictures of how to make it happen. They draw where all the walls, windows, and doors will go. Architects include the plumbing, electrical, and ventilation systems in their drawings. They provide exact measurements for every item. They decide what materials will be used.

Once the building is designed, and the engineers and builders begin to take over, the architects' job is not over, however. Architects frequently have to adjust their drawings. A feature that looks good on paper may not work at the construction site. Developers sometimes change their minds and want something in the original design altered. Unexpected problems can arise that require new calculations. Although they generally work in offices and at computers, architects sometimes visit construction sites. And because building contractors have deadlines, architects occasionally work overtime to help them meet those deadlines.

Because architects are the master planners of construction projects, they usually remain involved until the building is finished. All the teams involved in a project work from the architects' drawings, so the architects have to explain their vision to developers, contractors, suppliers, inspectors, and others involved in the building's construction.

Traditional architects are concerned primarily with how a building looks and how to build it within the budget the developer has. Green architects must also consider all the LEED criteria. They must think of energy, environment, and health issues in their designs.

Skills Needed

An architect is both an artist and a scientist. Architects have to be skilled in math, and they have to be good problem solvers. They do not have to draw well (a computer can now do that for them), but they have to be able to visualize how different design elements, components, and systems fit together and what the completed project will look like. They need to understand enough science and engineering so that they know that what they draw will actually work, stay standing, and be safe. At one time architects made their elaborate, precise drawings by hand, with paper and pencil. Now they use computer programs, specifically CAD—computer-aided design.

Preparation

Becoming an architect can take up to eight years of post–high school study. A person who wants to become an architect must first earn a bachelor's degree (usually takes four to five years) and possibly a master's degree (usually takes one to two years). In these college programs, students learn building design, graphic design, math and engineering concepts, physical science, and computer programming. After receiving a degree, the aspiring architect then completes an internship, working under the guidance of a licensed architect to learn the business. After a three-year internship, he or she can apply for a professional license.

Every state requires that architects be licensed. To be licensed, a person must pass a four-day-long examination. To keep their licenses, architects have to receive additional education every year, through workshops, seminars, college classes, or other forms of study. Green architects need to know the LEED criteria. Developers who want to build green projects hire architectural companies in which at least one of the architects is LEED-accredited.

Engineers

Like architects, engineers design things. They use math and science to figure out the technical details of the architect's plan. Different kinds of engineers design different parts of the building:

Civil engineers: Civil engineers plan the elements that have to do with the site, such as control of water, sewage, and traffic. They determine how deep to dig, where to put water lines, how much to slope a driveway, and similar calculations.

Mechanical engineers: Mechanical engineers design systems for heating, air-conditioning, and ventilation. In green building, mechanical

Green builders use equipment and techniques that create as little air pollution as possible. This earthmover has had its exhaust system retrofitted with filters to keep it from spewing pollutants into the air.

engineers oversee the generation and conservation of energy from renewable resources.

Electrical engineers: Electrical engineers design and test electrical systems. In green building, they develop controls for lighting and carbon dioxide (CO_2) monitoring.

Skills Needed

Engineers are problem solvers. Developers often have vague dreams of what they want to build, and architects visualize and draw in specific detail what that dream could look like in reality. Engineers look at the real-world conditions where the dream is to be built—the type of soil, climate, weather patterns, connections to city resources, local regulations, costs, expected use, etc.—and solve the problems those conditions create. They must be skilled in math, science, computers, and technology.

Preparation

To be an engineer in the building industry, a person must have at least a bachelor's degree in an engineering specialty—civil, mechanical, or electrical. Other types of engineering, such as aeronautical, geological, or nuclear, usually require a higher degree (a master's or a Ph.D.). The degree should be earned in a college or university with a good engineering program. A national organization—the Accreditation Board for Engineering and Technology (ABET)—examines college engineering programs and accredits those that are good. Getting into a top-notch engineering program requires good high school grades in math and science and high scores on college board exams like the SATs.

All states register engineers, but engineers do not have to have licenses. Many people who hire engineers, however—especially those involved in large projects—want to be sure they are of high quality. Obtaining a license is a way to clearly demonstrate your skill in the field. ABET offers a professional engineer license. To obtain this license and be recognized as a competent professional, a person has to have earned a degree from an ABET-accredited school, have four years of work experience in the field, and pass rigorous examinations.

It is possible, although not very common, to become an engineer without an engineering degree. People with degrees in math or a natural science who also have completed some engineering classes are sometimes able to get jobs as engineers. This is especially true if they have training in a very specific area where the need for knowledgeable and experienced people is high.

Engineering Technician

Some engineering tasks require creativity, experience, and broad knowledge of scientific principles. Others involve simple design and production. Often a professional engineer can solve a complex design problem, while a technician with less training can make the calculations and drawings the builder needs to implement that solution. In other words, a professional engineer might figure out the major design, and a technologist or technician might do the detail work. Many engineering companies have technologist or technician positions.

Colleges, community colleges, and technical schools have two-year and four-year programs that offer degrees in engineering technology. They teach less scientific theory and more hands-on applications of relevant theories. Graduates of these programs are sometimes called engineers, but they are not qualified to apply for professional engineer licensing. Nevertheless, they are among the most valuable and essential team members of any engineering firm.

Drafter

Architectural as well as engineering firms need skilled people to do detail work. That is essentially what drafters do. They draw up technical plans of all the aspects of the architect's or engineer's design. They provide exact measurements and specific procedures. Think of an architect's sketch as a large map and a drafter's drawing as zooming in on different places on the map. The architect's or engineer's plan is the big picture; the drafter's drawing gives the detailed directions for how to get there.

Drafters specialize in a specific area. Architectural drafters provide the details for the structural features of buildings. They may specialize further, working primarily in residential or commercial buildings, or in buildings made of concrete, steel, or wood. Civil drafters draw the specifics of water and sewage systems for civil engineers. Electrical drafters make elaborate diagrams for buildings' electrical systems. Mechanical drafters work out the details of the mechanical devices used in a project, such as the sensors that control energy usage. Drafters with knowledge of LEED criteria may specialize in green building.

Blueprints tell what is needed for the job and where it all goes. Blueprints give detailed pictures and exact measurements. Before work can start on a new building, city or county authorities must approve the blueprints.

High school courses in math, science, computer technology, and computer graphics are helpful preparation for careers in drafting. Good grades in these courses along with mechanical drawing skills, some knowledge of drafting standards, and a good grasp of CAD may be enough to land a drafting job. However, many employers look for a little more training. Technical schools, community colleges, and a few four-year colleges offer training programs in drafting. Some colleges award associate of arts degrees in drafting. Not all schools are of the same quality, so it is a good idea to check with prospective employers to find out what programs they recommend.

There is no drafter's license, but the American Design Drafting Association offers a certificate for people who pass a test demonstrating their knowledge of drafting concepts, terms, and standards. Employers usually do not require that their drafters are certified, but having a certificate does make someone stand out from all other job applicants.

Drafting is often viewed as a good entry into the fields of architecture and engineering. Drafters can move up from junior positions to intermediate and advanced levels. If they desire, they can continue their education and become engineering technicians, engineers, or architects.

Landscape Architect

Some people think of landscaping as a feature to be considered only after the building is complete. In green construction, however, landscaping is a big part of what makes a project eco-friendly. What vegetation will be on the property and where it will be located greatly affects the building's water and energy usage.

Like all architects, landscape architects are part artist, part engineer, and part scientist. They design an outdoor environment that both looks good and makes the best, most eco-friendly use of available resources. Landscape architects analyze the site's soil, climate, and weather. They study the way the land rises or slopes and where the sun strikes at what time of day. They research what plants are native to the location so they can use vegetation that requires no more water than the site receives naturally. Landscape architects work closely with engineers and building architects to design attractive features that will capture rainfall and

Landscape architects work with paper and pencil more than with plants. This architect is reviewing the design for a greenway, a corridor of open space, along the French Broad River in Asheville, North Carolina.

prevent excess storm water from running off the site. They position trees and arbors in ways that provide shade or insulation, helping to lower the building's energy needs.

Skills Needed

Good landscape architects require more than a love of plants and a good sense of design. They need computer skills, particularly CAD, to help them create and revise their designs. Because they have to present their design plans to developers and work with other professionals, they

One Person's Trash Is Another Person's Treasure

What do you do with twenty tons (20,000 kilograms) of wood you can't use? If no one else can use it either, how do you recycle that much wood? That is about how much waste wood the construction of the Gaia Hotel generated. The project manager sent it to a Wheelabrator Technologies waste-to-energy plant.

Wheelabrator operates facilities across the United States that turn waste into electrical and steam energy. It controls the emissions from the conversion process, and the result is clean energy. Its plant in Saugus, Massachusetts, can burn 1,500 tons (1.5 million kg) of trash each day, creating 14,000 kilowatts of electricity that can power forty thousand homes. Wheelabrator and similar companies recycle, in addition to wood, more than 450,000 tons (450 million kg) of glass, metals, paper, plastics, yard waste, and other materials. They generate enough electricity to power three million homes.

also need to be able to communicate well and know their way around multimedia slide presentation programs like PowerPoint.

Preparation

At a minimum, a landscape architect needs a bachelor's degree in landscape architecture, which takes four or five years of study. Many firms also require a master's degree, which requires an additional one to three years. The Landscape Architecture Accreditation Board of the

American Society of Landscape Architects accredits some colleges and universities to confer these degrees.

Forty-nine of the fifty United States require that landscape architects be licensed. Most use the Landscape Architect Registration Examination (LARE) to award licenses, but the requirements differ from state to state. A person who graduates from an accredited program, passes the LARE exam, and practices for three years under a licensed architect will meet the licensing requirements in most states.

Outlook for Planners

As long as structures need to be built or remodeled, there will be jobs in the architecture and engineering fields. Because interest in green building is growing, more jobs in these industries will require people with knowledge of sustainable building design. At the entry level, drafters and technicians can expect to earn between $27,000 and $70,000 per year. Engineers and architects, of course, are paid more—about $35,000 to $95,000. Starting salaries for engineers are among the highest for any college graduate. An engineer just graduating from college with a bachelor's degree will earn about $48,000. Architects usually start at about the same salary level.

Chapter Three

Green Builders

Although sustainable building is vastly different from traditional building, the practical day-to-day work of the builders does not appear to be very different. They work in much the same way as they would on any other project. They do incorporate a few additional techniques, and they use different materials. But the basic skills and knowledge that "green-collar" construction workers need are the same as they would need for any building project. The one exception to this is the project manager who oversees green building efforts.

Erecting a building takes "white-collar" workers who design the structures and "blue-collar" workers who turn the design into actual buildings. In sustainable construction, both are sometimes called "green-collar" workers.

Construction Project Manager

Sometimes called a superintendent, program manager, or supervisor, the construction project manager is the builder who is largely responsible for ensuring that the project is green. He or she is the point person for everything that happens during the actual building. Project managers direct, coordinate, and supervise the entire process from ground breaking to completion. They are responsible for the materials, the scheduling, the costs, the workers, and the overall quality.

The architect's plan specifies what materials are to be used, and the project manager has to decide where to get them and how to get them to the site. In green projects, the managers have to find materials made from either rapidly renewable resources or recycled content. They often purchase lumber that is certified as grown in a sustainable manner. The wood has a "chain of custody" certificate that tracks its history from the forest to the construction site, proving that it meets the LEED standard. All the materials carry documentation of their greenness. The project manager has to keep careful records of all this information . . . on recycled paper, of course.

Estimating time and cost is another important task for project managers. They look at all that must be done—from preparing the site and excavating for the foundation to laying carpet and installing cabinets—and decide on the proper sequence for each step and the amount of time each task should take. They figure in delays for bad weather and other problems that might arise.

Project managers do not do any of the building themselves, but they put together the teams that do. They hire

A project manager stands on a site that is ready for the building foundation. The tubes protruding from the ground are for the electrical, water, gas, and sewer lines that are beneath the building's foundation.

contractors who provide crews that do carpentry, plumbing, painting, electrical work, and other tasks. They coordinate the schedules of the different teams, try to keep the workers on those schedules, and watch to see that their work is good. When they are not at the construction site, they are on call, always available to answer questions from the many people they supervise and handle any problems that crop up at the site.

One of the primary responsibilities of a project manager on a green project is waste management. LEED points are earned if 50 percent or more of the waste from a construction site is recycled. A project manager either finds a way to use the leftover building materials or sees that they are taken to companies that recycle building waste.

Unlike traditional project managers, green project managers are responsible for maintaining healthy indoor air quality while the buildings are being constructed. Even with low-VOC materials, construction still creates dust and odors. Project managers keep the air inside the buildings as clean as possible by sealing ducts and equipment openings and covering carpets and other materials that might absorb toxins and emissions.

Skills Needed

Project managers need to understand architectural and engineering drawings and have good general knowledge of all aspects of building construction. Often an architect's plan will need to be adjusted to the actual circumstances and to unforeseen problems, and the project manager has to make those adjustments. Project managers need to possess the ability to solve problems and make decisions under pressure. They must be detail-oriented, able to communicate well, and able to build good relationships with different types of people, from engineers to laborers.

Preparation

The most important qualifications for a project manager position are experience in construction and skill in managing people. In green building, knowledge of LEED standards and procedures is also helpful. Although many project

How Eco-Friendly Are Traditional U.S. Buildings?

- Buildings use 37 percent of all energy produced.*
- Buildings consume 68 percent of all electricity produced.*
- Construction and deconstruction (demolition) waste account for 40 percent of all solid waste.*
- Outdoor uses, primarily landscaping, account for 30 percent of all water use.*
- Buildings account for 43 percent of all CO_2 emissions.**
- Every day 5 billion gallons (almost 19 billion liters) of potable water is used just for flushing toilets.*

*LEED-NC for New Construction Reference Guide, Version 2.2. Washington, DC: Green Building Council, 2005.

**Oak Ridge National Laboratory. *Towards a Climate-Friendly Built Environment.* Arlington, VA: Pew Center on Global Climate Change, 2005.

managers rise to their positions from the ranks of construction workers, developers and contractors often want the managers of their projects to have specialized education in the field. Some colleges offer bachelor's and master's degrees in construction management or building science. Some community colleges offer associate degrees in construction management and construction technology.

Although project managers do not need to be certified, two national organizations do offer certification. The

American Institute of Constructors awards two types of certifications: associate constructor and certified professional constructor. The Construction Management Association of America awards a certified construction manager certification. To receive one of these designations, a person must have professional experience and pass the organization's exams.

Site Preparers

One of the first teams the construction manager assembles is the one that gets the site ready for construction. These are the heavy equipment operators. They drive the bulldozers and other machines that clear the lot and grade the land to make it level. They operate excavators that scoop out and remove the earth to make room for buildings' foundations. They dig trenches for pipes and cables. They drive and operate forklifts, cranes, and other heavy equipment to move building materials to the right spots. They are responsible for the paving vehicles and equipment that spread, level, and smooth asphalt and cement for roads, driveways, and walkways.

Operating heavy equipment requires good health and good eye-hand-foot coordination. There is no educational requirement, and some find jobs as equipment operators without a high school diploma. Many people start out driving light equipment and advance with on-the-job training to the larger and more complex machines. However, more formal training is available, and employers often look for well-trained operators. Courses—including high school classes—in auto mechanics are helpful as

The first stage in the actual building of a structure is preparing the ground. Here, trees and dirt have been removed, and the soil has been leveled and compacted.

operators may also be required to service the equipment. Some vocational schools offer programs in operating specific equipment.

The International Union of Operating Engineers and the Associated General Contractors of America have apprenticeship programs that prepare people for these jobs. These programs consist of 144 hours of instruction and six thousand hours of on-the-job training. The programs take three years to complete, but apprentices are paid while they are working and are well qualified and more employable when their training is completed.

Building Crafts People

The actual construction of a building or a complex requires several teams, each with its own focus and skills:

> **Carpenters:** Carpenters cut and shape the wood or other building material and fasten the pieces together to form the building's frame. They need to be physically fit and have basic math skills.
>
> **Drywall installers:** Drywall installers attach drywall panels to the inside of the building frame. They fill the joints where the panels connect with a special compound and tape over the joint. In green construction, drywall installers use low-VOC materials.
>
> **Roofers:** Roofers install insulation and roofing materials. Green builders use a variety of roofing materials. They might install a "cool" roof made of a material that reflects the sun's heat more efficiently than a traditional roof. They might build a roof that is partially covered with solar panels. They may even construct a green roof, composed of soil, grasses, and other plants.
>
> **Plumbers:** Plumbers take care of everything that has to do with water. They install the water and waste disposal systems and the fixtures that access them: sinks, tubs, showers, and toilets. They install all the appliances that use water, such as dishwashers, washing machines, and water heaters. They connect the water system

This team is installing solar electric panels on the roof of a new home in Santa Monica, California. The panels will capture the sun's energy, store it, and convert it into electricity.

of the building to the city or municipal water and sewer lines that serve the project. The water system in a green building looks very different from a traditional system, as the plumbers incorporate the latest water conservation technology.

Electricians: Electricians install the wiring, switches, and outlets that will direct and control the flow of electricity throughout the building. They may also install cables and wiring for telephones, security systems, intercoms, and fire alarms. In a green building, the electricity may be generated by wind turbines, solar panels, or geothermal systems, rather than obtained from a city's power company. Yet electricians still have to route the electricity—no matter how it is generated or where it originates—to wherever it needs to go.

Solar panel installers: Solar panel installers are electricians, roofers, or other building contractors who specialize in installing and maintaining solar panels on building roofs.

In all the building crafts, people often begin as helpers to the more experienced workers. They haul materials, hold items in place, and clean up. Gradually they are given more responsibility and they become more skilled. Formal training is not always necessary, but it is helpful. High school classes in math, mechanical drawing, blueprint reading, and wood and metal shop are good preparation. Vocational schools and community colleges offer training programs. Some contractors, usually those with large projects, have apprenticeship programs that combine classroom instruction with paid on-the-job training. Most apprenticeships last three or four years.

Heating, Ventilation, and Air-Conditioning Technicians

The heating, ventilation, and air-conditioning system, usually referred to as HVAC, is the heart of energy conservation efforts in a green building. The HVAC system maintains comfort by controlling temperature, humidity, and air quality within the building. Traditional HVAC systems use forced air, which is heated or cooled and requires lots of energy, usually in the form of fossil fuels. Green systems, however, limit the use of forced air, relying more on natural means of climate control. Green HVAC technicians may install water supply lines in floors for radiant heating, waste-heat recovery systems to recirculate warm air, and occupancy sensors to turn off heating or cooling when they are not needed.

Green buildings have systems that monitor carbon dioxide (CO_2) levels in rooms. As people breathe, they take in oxygen and exhale CO_2. A room with too little oxygen and too much CO_2 is uncomfortable and unhealthy. Ventilation systems control the flow of fresh air (containing oxygen) into a room and the flow of "used" air (containing CO_2) out. HVAC technicians install CO_2 sensors to maintain the right balance automatically.

When HVAC technicians install systems in green buildings, they take precautions that are not required in traditional construction. They must maintain good air quality in the building as they work. So as they place ducting, before they connect the pieces together, they have to seal off the ends to prevent construction dust and pollutants from entering the interior of the building.

HVAC technicians need to have some knowledge of plumbing, electricity, and electronics. Unlike many in the building crafts who can enter the job market without specialized education, HVAC technicians generally need at least some formal training. Technical schools offer training

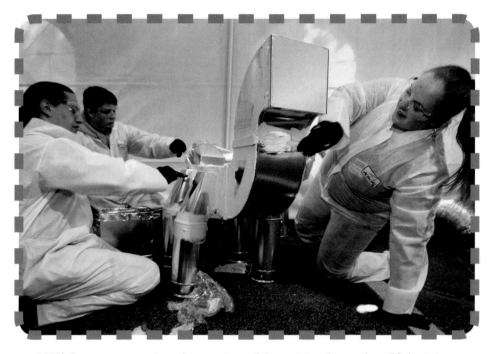

HVAC systems consist of a number of ducts joined together. If the joints are not airtight, the hot or cold air leaks out, wasting both energy and money. These technicians are training students on how to seal HVAC ducts and conduct air-leak tests.

programs that vary from six months to two years in length. In many states, HVAC installers and mechanics must be licensed. Licensing requirements vary, but all applicants must pass a test and most must serve a two- to five-year apprenticeship.

Outlook for Builders

As interest in ecology and conservation grows, so do the prospects for green builders. In addition to new construction, builders are needed to retrofit older, existing buildings to make them more green. Already-built homes, offices, and other buildings are being modified to incorporate energy- and water-saving features.

Construction project managers who oversee green building projects generally earn between $56,000 and $100,000. In addition to their salaries, they may earn bonuses based on the amount of money they can save on the project, and they may have use of a company vehicle.

Other builders typically are paid by the hour. Heavy equipment operators and HVAC technicians make $14 to $30 per hour. Wages for workers in the various construction crafts range from $13 to $35 per hour, with plumbers and electricians at the higher end.

Chapter Four

Green Consultants

In the building industry, many green jobs are simply traditional "white-collar" jobs (architects, engineers) or "blue-collar" jobs (building crafts people), with special attention paid to eco-friendly materials, technologies, and techniques. However, some jobs are focused exclusively on sustainable construction. These are the people the planners and builders consult as they learn how to adapt traditional practices to green purposes.

The project manager of the MGM Mirage CityCenter, a megaresort in Las Vegas, inspects one of the center's buildings. Eight architects designed the "city within a city," incorporating many energy-saving features, including an on-site power generation plant.

LEED Professionals

The gold standard for measuring greenness is currently LEED certification. A builder who wants to prove exactly how environmentally friendly his or her project is will want to earn LEED points, or credits. Most eco-conscious builders want to go beyond the minimum number of LEED credits and have their structures certified as silver, gold, or plati-

The platinum rating is the highest level of LEED certification from the U.S. Green Building Council.

num. The LEED rating system is very precise, and builders must meet strict standards and scrupulously document their actions. Meeting the criteria takes careful calculation of many factors. If a standard is missed by even a fraction of a percent, no point is awarded. Calculating and recording the recycled content of building materials, the VOC level of paints, the water flow rate of a shower, and many, many other facets of the building's materials, systems, and operations is a job for professionals.

Builders of large projects often hire LEED-accredited professionals to help them reach and maintain

"Casa Nueva," a municipal building in Santa Barbara County, California, features roof sails that lower the temperature of the roof, its equipment, and the intake air, reducing the energy needed for cooling the building's interior.

LEED standards. LEED certifiers advise builders on which materials qualify for the LEED credits. They explain how specific LEED criteria apply to builders' projects. And they guide builders through the certification process. Simply having a LEED-accredited professional on the construction team earns the project one point (in the Innovation in Design category).

People who work in different parts of the building industry often decide to become LEED professionals. Anyone with good knowledge of and experience in green building can take a test and become a LEED-accredited professional. The U.S. Green Building Council offers full-day and half-day workshops, online courses, and "webinars" (Web-hosted seminars) to teach what an accredited professional needs to know. People who are interested can download a handbook and an exam preparation guide from the Green Building Certification Institute Web site. They can also register for the test at this site.

For a number of years, a general accredited professional certificate was the only LEED-related certificate offered. It indicated that the holder of the certificate had demonstrated knowledge and skill in green design, construction, and operations, and knew LEED standards. Today, accredited professionals specialize in various areas. For this reason, the certificate now indicates the professional's specific expertise: building design and construction, interior design and construction, operations and maintenance, homes, or neighborhood development.

The average salary for a beginning LEED-accredited professional is $54,000.

Community college students in Iowa learn about green building by helping to build an energy-efficient house. They learn through a combination
of classroom instruction and field experience.

Commissioning Agent

The purpose of sustainable construction is not merely to have eco-friendly building practices. It is also to create structures that continue to be green in their ongoing operations, for the duration of the buildings' lives. Builders achieve this through the additional step of commissioning. The LEED Reference Guide defines commissioning as "the process of ensuring that systems are designed, installed, functionally tested, and capable of being operated and maintained" as they were designed. In other words, commissioning is the same as quality control. It is the step that ensures that the building was not only built green, but also operates green. This oversight process is carried out by commissioning agents.

Commissioning agents are basically LEED-accredited professionals who focus on energy efficiency, water conservation, and air quality. They are involved from the building's early planning stages through to the building's completion and actual operation. In the design phase, commissioning agents draft a plan describing how each system will be tested. As construction progresses, they monitor how well the systems are doing what they are supposed to do. When the building is finished, but before it is in use, the agents check and report on the performance of the systems. After a year of operation, they test the systems again.

Commissioning agents need to have several years of experience with energy, water, and HVAC systems of buildings. They are often mechanical engineers who have obtained certification as LEED-accredited professionals.

Energy Modeler

One of the ways to achieve one of the primary goals of green building—energy conservation—is through energy use simulation. Builders need to consider different options and decide which provide the greatest energy savings for the cost. Would the building use less energy if it faced north rather than east? Would curved or squared windows work better? How much insulation is enough, and what kind would be most efficient and eco-friendly? Energy modelers use computer programs to compare all the different possibilities.

Energy modeling is part of the initial design phase. The energy modeler considers several designs. He or she then runs computer simulations of the amount of energy saved in the operation of the building under each of these designs. Computer modeling programs are necessary because each design has many components, and the various components of the different designs can be combined in a multitude of ways. A computer can calculate and shuffle all these variables in mere seconds, whereas a human would take days and weeks to perform the same complicated calculations and comparisons. Based on the results of these projections, the computer modeler makes recommendations to the architect and engineers who create the final plan.

Energy modelers are usually mechanical engineers. They are very often LEED-accredited professionals and part of the engineer team that consults the project manager throughout the entire construction project. They must have excellent computer skills, and they must be able to explain highly technical information to people with far less understanding of science and computers.

Energy raters measure a building's energy efficiency with tools such as this home heat aid. It takes infrared readings to measure temperature and detect heat leaks.

Home Energy Auditor

Buildings can leak energy, usually in the form of lost heating or cooling. Hot or warm air can escape through ducts that are not tight and through gaps where walls and floors or ceilings meet. Energy auditors, or raters, inspect buildings for these energy leaks. They test not just the ductwork, but the entire building. They use computer programs to analyze the leaks they discover and to estimate how much energy and money could be saved if the leaks were closed.

Energy auditors can also help in the design of buildings. Builders of smaller projects, such as a single home, may not want to pay an engineer to design the building. They may not be seeking LEED certification but may simply want to have a home that is energy efficient. These contractors may hire an energy rater to look at their building plans and predict how well the home will keep its energy. The energy rater scores the plans according to a rating system developed by the Residential Energy Services Network (RESNET), giving it a Home Energy Rating score (HERS). The energy rater may suggest measures that will improve the building's energy efficiency. During construction and after completion, the energy rater may test the building again and assign it a revised HERS score.

Contractors who are retrofitting existing homes to make them more energy efficient also hire energy auditors. The energy auditor tests the home, performs computer analyses, gives the home a rating, and makes recommendations for better efficiency.

Home energy auditors are certified through companies authorized by RESNET. To become an energy

Green Environments Boost Performance

People are healthier and perform better in green buildings. Studies have shown that in some green buildings:

- Absenteeism went down 15 percent
- Incidence of respiratory illness went down 9 to 20 percent
- Student performance in math improved 20 percent
- Worker productivity increased 2 to 16 percent

Source: Alex Wilson, "Productivity and Green Buildings." *Environmental Building News*, October 1, 2004.

auditor, a person must pass an exam and perform three rating inspections and reports under the guidance of a certified rater. Training is not absolutely necessary, but the test is difficult. RESNET-accredited training centers offer intensive weeklong courses that explain the scientific principles upon which ratings are based and provide opportunities to practice conducting energy inspections. Most auditors have their own businesses and purchase their own equipment. Start-up costs can be as high as $5,100 to $8,500. This consists of $1,200 to $2,500 for training, $3,600 to $4,500 for equipment, and $300 to $1,500 for fees.

Outlook

In February 2009, the U.S. Green Building Council cited a study that predicted that the green building industry would more than double by 2013. That means that the demand for green consultants is growing rapidly. Green consultants are generally engineers or construction project managers who have the experience and credentials to advise green building teams. Their salaries are typically the same as or a little higher than those for engineer and project manager positions.

Unlike engineering consultants, energy auditors do not need more than a high school education to begin working. Therefore their pay is lower. Because they are usually in business for themselves, they are paid by the job. Typically, energy auditors begin at around $10 per hour.

Chapter Five
Green Finishers

If they are going to sell, sustainable buildings need to not only be eco-friendly, they also must look good and be comfortable, just like any other new building. That's the job of the finishing teams. Painters, tile workers, landscapers, and interior designers put on the finishing touches. Though primarily concerned with a building's appearance, the finishers, like the designers and builders, also need to consider energy efficiency, water conservation, and air quality.

Jamie and Isaac Salm, founders of Mio Design, a sustainable design firm, create a wide range of products for the home and the office that use eco-friendly materials. Here, they are testing a new design for a lamp.

Painting a green building does not require skills that are any different from those needed to paint any other building. The difference is in the paint. Environmentally friendly paints contain few or no VOCs.

Painters

Green painters are no different from traditional painters. They use sprayers, rollers, and brushes to apply paint and other finishes to a building's exterior and interior walls. But the paint used on green buildings is different. It must be "low-emitting." That is, the VOC content must be below the level established by LEED. This is the case for the paint, primer, and any sealers and floor coatings.

Low-VOC paints do not have the characteristic paint smell. They are healthier than traditional paints for the painters as well as for the building occupants. By using low-VOC paint, the painting team helps the building maintain good air quality.

Most painters do not have formal training. They begin as painters' helpers, carrying materials, preparing surfaces, and doing other small jobs. They gradually learn about paints and how to mix and apply them. Starting with simple jobs, they work their way to the larger jobs as they hone their skills. Some technical schools offer training and apprenticeships, but most painters learn on the job. They start at wages around $10 per hour and can advance to about $25.

Landscapers

The grounds around a building, far from being an afterthought, are actually an integral part of any green construction project. A landscape architect designs the area, and landscapers fill it in with vegetation, earthworks, and ornamentation. They contour, or shape, the land according to the landscape architect's plan. This shaping controls where water will flow and where it will collect. Landscapers plant trees, shrubs, flowers, and grasses. If the plants are to be watered by the building's gray water or a rain collection facility, the landscapers install the lines that will carry that water. They may also install walkways, fountains, and other decorative items. Landscapers on a green project differ from traditional landscapers in the way they maintain the grounds. For example, they do not use chemical pesticides, which are harmful to the environment, and they plant vegetation that won't require a lot of watering.

The need for landscapers, particularly green landscapers, appears to be growing faster than many other jobs. They can earn from $10 to $20 per hour.

Tile Setters

Tile setters apply hard tile to floors, walls, ceilings, and countertops. In a green building, tile setters use tiles made of recycled materials. Unlike traditional tiles, these tiles are often not uniform in size, which may present a slight challenge to the green tile setter. Still, the work is much like that in any other building. The tile setters lay the tiles out in a pattern, place spacers between them to keep the pattern even, and cut them to fit around obstacles such as pipes. Then they apply, or "set," them with a thin coat of low-VOC adhesive.

The greatest growth in green tile-setting jobs is in large-scale projects. Stores, schools, hospitals, and restaurants use tile. And the number of major stores, companies, and

Landscapers on a green project use plants that are native to the area, so they require little if any water other than what they receive naturally through rain and other precipitation.

institutions that are interested in sustainable construction is growing. Tile setters in these projects earn between $13 and $25 per hour.

Carpet Layers and Floor Finishers

The people who put the final touches on the floors of green buildings are traditional craftspeople who use eco-friendly products. Carpet layers, who cut and install flooring, use carpet in which the fibers, the backing, and the pads are all made of recycled materials. The glue they use to adhere the carpet to the floor must emit very few VOCs. The absence of VOCs in the adhesive means an absence of new carpet smell in the rooms.

Laying carpet is a physically demanding job. Installers often lift and carry heavy rolls of carpet. They work in a kneeling position with bent backs for hours. In the past, demand for carpet layers was high because the physical demands cause people to change jobs, creating frequent openings for new workers. However, carpet is becoming less popular as a floor covering, so the number of jobs available is actually declining. Those who choose this career can expect to make $12 to $25 per hour.

Interior Designers

Interior designers put the finishing touches on every project. They are the ones who add furniture, wall decor, window coverings, and lighting. Some also plan architectural details of the interior spaces of the building, such as built-in bookcases or planter boxes, kitchen counters, window

This tile setter is using tiles made of recycled materials to decorate a kitchen countertop and backsplash in a home. He is affixing the tiles with low-VOC-emitting adhesive.

seats, or arched doorways. In a green building, every item the decorator adds should be eco-friendly.

Primarily, that means three things. The item must be: (a) made of rapidly renewable resources or salvaged or recycled materials; (b) able to be recycled when it is no longer usable; and (c) free of VOCs and other harmful pollutants. Green interior designers need to order furniture from companies that manufacture sustainable houseware furnishings.

Interior designers need to not only be creative, they must also read about and keep up with changing trends. They need to understand art and design principles and be able to use CAD programs to create plans. Green designers must have a good understanding of eco-friendly wood products and fabrics.

Community colleges and design schools offer two- and three-year training programs and an associate of arts degree. Some four-year colleges and universities have bachelor's degree programs in interior design. These are often offered in the art, architecture, or home economics departments. A degree is required for most entry-level interior design positions.

Almost half of the states in the United States require that interior designers be registered or licensed. The National Council for Interior Design Accreditation confers the licenses. To get a license, a person must have six years of education. At least two of these years must be education after high school. The person must also have experience in the field and pass a written test.

Interior designers can specialize by type of building (hospital, office, hotel, restaurant, house, apartment, theater,

Beth Bailey salvages old materials from homes. She is standing next to a fireplace built with bricks from an old cottage that once stood on the current site of this house in Franklin Township, Ohio.

etc.) or type of design (such as American country, art deco, art nouveau, French country, craftsman, mission, neoclassical, etc.). Some specialize in green design. The job market for interior designers in most specialties is growing, and the market for green designers is no exception. Many companies and individuals who are willing to pay for a design consultant to help them decorate are happy to decorate with items that are kind to the environment. A green interior designer can expect to earn $32,000 to $78,000 per year.

The Future of Green Building and Planning

Green building is the new frontier in construction. It is growing at a faster rate than other segments of the building industry. *Forbes Magazine* reported that green

An Environmentally Friendly Chair

The Steelcase Company has partnered with McDonough Braungart Design Chemistry to create the Think Chair. Steelcase advertises the product as "conceived, developed, and produced for maximum sustainability." Of the materials used in making the chair, 41 percent are recycled, and all materials are harmless to the environment and VOC-free. It is manufactured with minimal waste and energy consumption. Its light weight (32 pounds; 14.5 kg) means little fuel is needed to ship it. When the user is finished with the chair, it can be taken apart in five minutes with simple tools and recycled; it is 99 percent recyclable.

construction has been steadily growing at a rate of about 5 percent per year for several years. In 2007, eco-friendly construction in the United States was a $12 billion business. Sustainable building is good for the environment, good for the economy, and good for people's health. Americans typically spend 90 percent of their time indoors, and the more buildings there are that have good indoor air quality, the healthier people will be. Developers and builders are realizing that constructing environmentally friendly homes, offices, and other buildings pays dividends in cost savings, water and energy conservation, and improved health for years to come. Careers in green building and planning can provide solid incomes and advancement opportunities for individuals and great benefits for communities.

Someone has to dream, someone has to design, someone has to build those green buildings. One of those "someones" could be you!

Glossary

adhesive Something used to stick two materials to each other.

apprenticeship Training program in which a person works under the guidance and supervision of a skilled worker, learning the trade and becoming gradually skilled in it.

biofuel Fuel made by converting plant materials such as grasses, trees, and crops to heat energy.

CAD Computer-aided design; computer software that enables drafters, architects, and other designers to draw and change designs.

CO_2 (carbon dioxide) A gas we exhale when we breathe; a greenhouse gas emitted by the burning of fossil fuels that traps heat in the atmosphere. This greenhouse effect is resulting in global warming and climate change.

ecosystem A basic unit of nature that consists of living organisms (plants, animals, and microorganisms) in an area functioning together with all of the nonliving physical factors of the environment.

fossil fuels Carbons or hydrocarbons found in the earth's crust that were formed by pressure being exerted over centuries on the remains of plants and animals that died in prehistoric times. When these fuels are burned, they release chemical energy to power machines and vehicles, but they also emit harmful gases and pollutants.

geothermal power Energy generated from heat stored deep in the earth.

gray water Household wastewater that has not come into contact with toilet waste and has not been treated to purify it. Usually, it consists of water from bathtubs, showers, washbasins, and clothes washers, but not from kitchen sinks or dishwashers.

HERS score Home Energy Rating score; a measure of a home's energy efficiency measured against typical homes of the same size in the same area.

landfill Site where waste materials are disposed of by burying them; sometimes called a dump.

LEED Leadership in Energy and Environmental Design; the most widely used green building rating system in the United States, developed by the U.S. Green Building Council.

permeable pavement Asphalt or concrete that permits water to pass through it into the ground.

potable Refers to water that is suitable for drinking.

power grid Lines and connections through which electric power flows from power suppliers to utility users.

radiant heating/cooling Method of heating or cooling a room in which a surface is heated or cooled, usually by piping warm or cold water in floors or walls, and the heat then spreads out, or radiates into the room.

rapidly renewable resource A resource that can be renewed, or replaced, within ten years.

renewable resource A naturally occurring item that can be replenished.

retrofit To remodel an existing building in order to add water and energy conservation features and other eco-friendly upgrades.

sensor Device that detects the presence of some item, such as heat, motion, or the people in a room.

sustainable building Method of planning and constructing buildings that conserves and restores renewable resources and has as little as possible negative impact on the environment.

volatile organic compound (VOC) A carbon-based chemical that vaporizes under normal conditions, sending harmful gases into the atmosphere.

webinar Teaching method in which a teacher presents material over the Internet to a group of students who sign in to the "class"; an interactive Internet seminar.

For More Information

American Institute of Architects
1735 New York Avenue NW
Washington, DC 20006-5292
Web site: http://www.aia.org
This is a professional association of architects.

American Society of Civil Engineers
1801 Alexander Bell Drive
Reston, VA 20191-4400
Web site: http://www.asce.org
This is a professional organization for civil engineers. Its
    Web site has a page for "Kids and Careers."

Canadian Council of Professional Engineers
180 Elgin Street, Suite 1100
Ottawa, ON K2P 2K3
Canada
(613) 232-2474
Web site: http://www.engineerscanada.ca/e
This national organization of the twelve provincial and
    territorial associations regulates the practice of engi-
    neering and the licensing of engineers in Canada.

Canadian Society of Landscape Architects
P.O. Box 13594
Ottawa, ON K2K 1X6
Canada

(866) 781-9799
Web site: http://csla.ca
This is a national organization of landscape architects
   of Canada.

Green Building Certification Institute
1800 Massachusetts Avenue NW, Suite 300
Washington, DC 20036
Web site: http://www.gbci.org
This institute provides information about how to become
   a LEED-accredited professional.

Institute of Electrical and Electronics Engineering, Inc.
1828 L Street NW, Suite 1202
Washington, DC 20036-5104
Web site: http://www.ieee.org
This is a professional association of electrical engineers.
   Web site is helpful for anyone interested in the
   advancement of technology.

Junior Engineering Technical Society (JETS)
JETS Guidance Project
1420 King Street, Suite 405
Alexandria, VA 22314-2794
Web site: http://www.jets.org
The mission of this national nonprofit educational asso-
   ciation is to increase interest in, and awareness of,
   engineering and technology-based careers.

Residential Energy Services Network
P.O. Box 4561
Oceanside, CA 92052-4561

(760) 806-3448
Web site: http://www.natresnet.org
This national organization sets quality standards for
    building energy performance certification and certifies
    home energy raters.

Royal Architectural Institute of Canada
330-55 Murray Street
Ottawa, ON K1N 5M3
Canada
(613) 241-3600
Web site: http://www.raic.org/index_e.htm
This is a professional association for architects in Canada.

Society of American Registered Architects
305 East 46th Street
New York, NY 10017
Web site: http://sara-national.org
This is a professional association for architects.

Web Sites

Due to the changing nature of Internet links, Rosen
Publishing has developed an online list of Web sites
related to the subject of this book. This site is updated
regularly. Please use this link to access this list:

http://www.rosenlinks.com/gca/build

For Further Reading

Apel, Melanie Ann. *Careers in the Building and Construction Trades*. New York, NY: The Rosen Publishing Group, 2005.

Cassio, Jim, and Alice Rush. *Green Careers: Choosing Work for a Sustainable Future*. Gabriola Island, BC, Canada: New Society Publishers, 2009.

Chiras, Dan. *The New Ecological Home: A Complete Guide to Green Building Options*. White River Junction, VT: Chelsea Green Publishing Co., 2004.

Crosten, Glenn. *75 Green Businesses You Can Start to Make Money and Make a Difference*. Irvine, CA: Entrepreneur Media, Inc., 2008.

Environmental Careers Organization. *The ECO Guide to Careers That Make a Difference: Environmental Work for a Sustainable World*. Washington, DC: Island Press, 2004.

Everett, Melissa. *Making a Living While Making a Difference: Conscious Careers in an Era of Interdependence*. Gabriola Island, BC, Canada: New Society Publishers, 2007.

Freed, Eric Corey. *Green Building and Remodeling for Dummies*. Hoboken, NJ: Wiley Publishing, Inc., 2008.

Greenland, Paul R., and Annamarie L. Sheldon. *Career Opportunities in Conservation and the Environment*. New York, NY: Checkmark Books, 2007.

Hunter, Malcolm L., Jr., et al. *Saving the Earth as a Career: Advice on Becoming a Conservation Professional*. Malden, MA: Blackwell Publishing, 2007.

Llewellyn, A. Bronwyn, James P. Hendrix, and K. C.
    Golden. *Green Jobs: A Guide to Eco-Friendly
    Employment.* Avon, MS: Adams Media Corp., 2008.
McNamee, Gregory. *Careers in Renewable Energy:
    Get a Green Energy Job.* Masonville, CO: PixyJack
    Press, 2008.
Yudelson, Jerry. *Green Building A to Z: Understanding
    the Language of Green Building.* Gabriola Island, BC,
    Canada: New Society Publishers, 2007.
Yudelson, Jerry. *The Green Building Revolution.*
    Washington, DC: Island Press, 2007.

Bibliography

Fasulo, Mike, and Paul Walker. *Careers in the Environment*. New York, NY: McGraw Hill, 2007.

Georgia Municipal Association. "Top 10 Green Building Trends for 2009." February 6, 2009. Retrieved February 17, 2009 (http://www.gmanet.com/ MDR.aspx?CNID=35666).

Llewellyn, A. Bronwyn, James P. Hendrix, and K. C. Golden. *Green Jobs: A Guide to Eco-Friendly Employment*. Avon, MS: Adams Media Corp., 2008.

McNamee, Gregory. *Careers in Renewable Energy: Get a Green Energy Job*. Masonville, CO: PixyJack Press, 2008.

Residential Energy Services Network. *What and How of a Home Energy Rater*. Retrieved February 22, 2009 (http://www.natresnet.org/rater/What_and_How_ of_a_Rater.pdf).

Steelcase. *Environmental Think* (brochure). Retrieved February 22, 2009 (http://www.steelcase.com/na/ files/dyn/51b10a138c395a95524647c4af8c0dbc/ 04-0011852.pdf).

U.S. Department of Labor, Bureau of Labor Statistics. *Occupational Outlook Handbook, 2008-2009*. St. Paul, MN: JIST, 2008.

U.S. Green Building Council. "Green Building Facts: Green Building by the Numbers." February 2009. Retrieved February 22, 2009 (http://www.usgbc. org/ShowFile.aspx?DocumentID=3340).

U.S. Green Building Council. *LEED-NC for New Construction Reference Guide* (Version 2.2). Washington, DC: U.S. Green Building Council, 2005.

Wheelabrator Technologies. "What Is Waste-to-Energy?" 2008. Retrieved February 22, 2009 (http://www.wheelabratortechnologies.com/wte_what_it_is.htm).

Wingfield, Brian. "For Job Market, Green Means Growth." *Forbes*, July 3, 2007. Retrieved May 2009 (http://www.forbes.com/2007/07/02/environment-economy-jobs-biz_cx_bw_0703green_greenjobs.html).

Yudelson, Jerry. *Green Building A to Z: Understanding the Language of Green Building.* Gabriola Island, BC, Canada: New Society, 2007.

Index

About the Author

Ann Byers is a youth worker who helps high school students and young adults learn life skills. For this book, she worked with Cory Walczak, a construction project manager for green hotels in California.

Photo Credits

Cover (front, back) David Paul Morris/Getty Images; p. 1 (left) © www.istockphoto.com/Scott Feuer; p. 1 (right) © www.istockphoto.com/Vasko Miokovic; pp. 4–5 © www.istockphoto.com/José Luis Gutiérrez; p. 8 © Dave Darnell/The Commercial Appeal/Landov; pp. 11, 13, 15, 35, 44, 46, 47, 50, 53 © AP Images; p. 20 spnphotostwo/Newscom.com; p. 24 Robert Nickelsberg/Getty Images; p. 28 © www.istockphoto.com/roger lecuyer; p. 30 Philip Schermeister/National Geographic/Getty Images; p. 33 © www.istockphoto.com/Pamela Moore; p. 39 © www.istockphoto.com/e_rasmus; p. 41 David McNew/Getty Images; p. 48 ambphotos/Newscom.com; pp. 57, 65 krtphotoslive/Newscom.com; p. 58 © www.istockphoto.com/Linda Macpherson; p. 61 © www.istockphoto.com/Melissa Carroll; p. 63 Chris Martinez/La Opinion/Newscom.com.

Designer: Sam Zavieh; Photo Researcher: Amy Feinberg